London Travel Guide:

The Ultimate London, United Kingdom Tourist Trip Travel Guide

By

Angela Pierce

Table of Contents

Introduction 5

Chapter 1. Location Details 7

Chapter 2. Weather 8

Chapter 3. Fascinating Places to Visit in London 10

Chapter 4. Bars and Restaurants 23

Chapter 5. Night Life in London 27

Chapter 6. Shopping in The City of London 29

Chapter 7. Hotels in London 30

Final Words 31

Thank You Page 32

London Travel Guide: The Ultimate London, United Kingdom Tourist Trip Travel Guide

By Angela Pierce

© Copyright 2015 Angela Pierce

Reproduction or translation of any part of this work beyond that permitted by section 107 or 108 of the 1976 United States Copyright Act without permission of the copyright owner is unlawful. Requests for permission or further information should be addressed to the author.

This publication is designed to provide accurate and authoritative information in regard to the subject matter covered. This work is sold with the understanding that the publisher is not engaged in rendering legal, accounting, or other professional services. If legal advice or other expert assistance is required, the services of a competent professional person should be sought.

First Published, 2015

Printed in the United States of America

Introduction

London is one of the oldest cities of our modern world and seats her majesty the Queen of England since it is the capital city of the United Kingdom. It also happens to be one of the busiest and popular destinations for tourists around the world. It is located on the banks of the River Thames and is a wonderful place with great heritage spots all around. Though London is a modern day city with its dazzling night lights, hoard of crowds, this bustling city maintains a strong connection to its past. The glorious past of a colonialist country that had the elites of the world making London their home!

Amongst the innumerable Victorian structures, London is a very cosmopolitan city which is today a melting pot of various cultures considering a large immigrant population here. But this very cultural mix makes London a gastronomical paradise for those who love food. You can also dig into some traditional English dishes that are available widely and makes the place outstanding in terms of the destination details.

London is a home to many attractions of tourist interests. The best museums and the world renowned heritage spots in the city are really wonderful and make the real impact on tourists who come to this city. It is also one of the important financial centers in Europe. As a tourist there is a lot to see and do here. Right from taking strolls in the alleys of Victorian Era to letting yourself loose in a night club, London gives you all this and more!

Chapter 1. Location Details

There are three hills that surrounds the city and they are the Parliament, Addington, and Primrose Hill. All of them have a low height and thus they add beauty to the city that is located just by the side of the Thames. The marshlands found in and around the city make it even more beautiful and are also one of the key attractions for travelers. There are several bridges that not only connect one side to the other but they deserve a few looks owing to their architectural sensibilities. Due to the topography of the place and the perfect weather condition, the night life of the place is growing fast. The night comes alive here in various world class night clubs that also define the modern culture of this city.

Chapter 2. Weather

The climatic condition of the City is ideal for the tourists especially during summers. The winter season is quite chilly and dips to freezing points but the summer season through autumn is beautiful. In fact winter season witnesses strong winds that make it very difficult to venture out after sunset. The holiday season around Christmas of course is an entirely different story when loads of revelers can be seen taking to the streets and atmosphere becomes supremely celebratory. It never gets hot here and the weather is pleasant throughout except during winters. The best thing about the climate here is the temperature difference and the differentiation of the seasons. There are three seasons in the state and they are broadly, the summer, winter and the rainy season. The most important part here is that there is nothing called spring or autumn separately. The spring and autumn are included in the summer and the winter and thus the weather condition of the place is pleasant and ideal for all the dwellers.

Months of October and March are the best time and ideal for travel purposes. Most of the travelers reach here from different parts of the world in these two months. Generally the rainy season is avoided by the tourists, since the condition of the city becomes poor at that time.

Chapter 3. Fascinating Places to Visit in London

London is a place where modern and historical heritage amalgamate to give a serene and artistic environment for the tourists and the residents. Most of the places are affordable to visit. The best of attractions that will make your visit a memorable one have been handpicked for you and mentioned in detail here.

British Museum

The British Museum is a place where the significant transition of time is seen from traditional historical times to modern age. There are several works which are structured inside the British museum. Rosetta stone, the sculptures of Parthenon and the mummies of Africa are the most prominent ones that are included in the collection of the museum. This place also consists of important pre-historical carvings that date back to old civilizations of the world.

Natural History Museum

This is one of the most fascinating places to visit in London. Inside the National History Museum, there is a huge hall in the centre which exhibits the humongous skeleton of a dinosaur. The Museum is full of informative content that includes age old fossils of different kinds of animals and birds. Worlds' largest, tallest and the rarest animals are exhibited in this museum. Several other interesting animals such as an ancient species of spider and a big blue whale are also on display here. Information regarding all the exhibits is properly given along a display board beside the exhibit animals or models.

Science Museum

The scientific developments and research works of eminent researchers and scientists from all over the world are placed inside this museum. The Science Museum in London is a place where the architecture of the scientific development is placed in order of ascending timeline. If you want to know about the inventions and discoveries dating back from the 16th century to the 21st century, this is the most appropriate place to visit in the heart of London. Here the earlier experimental models of inventions are placed for the purpose of exhibition. Going around the museum you will find yourself travelling with the time from the past to the present. The science museum also presents the futuristic models of technology.

Victoria and Albert Museum

This museum is a visual treat for those who have an appreciation for arts and crafts. Victoria and Albert museum exhibits the old artifacts from all over the world, some of them as old as 3000 years! The museum better known as V&A deals in designs that are responsible for the evolution of arts through the ages. It celebrates the creations of mankind and the artistic side of human evolution by exhibiting some of the greatest artifacts of all times. This museum places a huge collection of cultural heritage within itself in form of sculptures from all around the world. Other artifacts and showpieces designed by artists and craftsman are also present. Some of the greatest works of paintings, wood craft, furniture, and textiles are also displayed for the general public.

Greenwich Royal Museum

This is the largest maritime museum in the world. Inside the museum you can find some of the greatest works of the maritime field. The devices that the international maritime organizations deal with and use are displayed for exhibition. Amongst all the interesting things that one can see inside this museum is the famous house of Queen. This is a place of historical importance. The museum is located on very serene lowland. The museum itself looks like an ancient monument. One can also stand along the Prime Meridian which is located at the Observatory of the royal museum Greenwich.

Madame Tussauds Wax Museum

Madame Tussaud is a wax museum in the heart of London which is named after the famous wax sculptor Marie Tussaud. Wax statues of different personalities from all around the world can be found inside this museum. This art gallery has the statues of all the influential people from all across the world dealing in the fields of arts, science, cinema, politics and many others. You can click a photo with Shakespeare and Einstein at the same time. You may choose to stand with the Hollywood star Brad Pitt or strike a pose with the god of cricket Sachin Tendulkar.

Tower of London

Amongst the most famous and beautiful buildings in London is the Tower of London. This building has a rich history of 900 years. To take a tour of this striking monument you have to take the help of the Yeoman Warders. This building is considered to be one of the most magnificent creations of the world. This building is rich in architectural designs. This old building has been a royal palace in the past and later a place where prisoners were confined and executed. The Tower of London used to be place for storing jewels as this was considered to be safest place in London in olden days. There are towers all around the four corners of this huge building. It looks like a huge fort protected from all side by huge brick walls. You may look up at the towers and get amazed by the designs that are engraved on to the walls of these towers.

London Eye

The most prominent and visible structure in whole of London is the London eye. It is a ferris wheel similar to cycle's rim and defines city's skyline. This is probably one of the largest structures in the heart of London and is located besides the Thames. This wheel is also known as the Millennium wheel. There are 32 capsules present in this structure and each can accommodate up to 25 people. Tourists generally embark this capsule to grab a breathtaking view of the London. The wheel rotates for duration of 30 minutes and all of the 55 magnificent landmarks in London can viewed from this capsule. This London eye attracts several tourists from all around the world.

Tate Modern

This is a British museum of modern and contemporary art located on the bank of river Thames. The building that houses the museum used to be a power station in earlier times. The Museum has a unique shape. Inside the museum there are several galleries that house numerous restaurants. This restaurant serves delicacies of different cuisine. The galleries of this museum offer a fantastic view of the city of London. Tate museum looks more beautiful and stunning at night when the whole of the building is lighted up with colorful lights. The colors of the walls change and thus the contrasting reflection of lights from the river Thames offers a very attractive view for the travelers and tourist in the evening. The appearance and the decoration of the museum as seen in the night reflects the modern and contemporary art this museum deals with.

National Gallery

The National Gallery is an art museum in the city of Westminster, Central London. This museum is located in the Trafalgar square. This is museum where more than 2300 paintings from all over the world with some dating back to 13th century are displayed. Most of the other paintings that are displayed for exhibition are from European countries. The vast space of the national gallery in London is filled up with paintings from Western Europe. The paintings range from the 13th century to 19th century. The most remarkable paintings that are housed inside the national gallery are the works of Leonardo da Vinci, Vincent Van Gogh, Renoir, and Boticelli. Arts students and enthusiast from all over the world visit this museum all around the year to get some inspiration from the exhibited paintings.

Tower Bridge

The tower bridge over the river Thames in London is one of the most popular bridges known by the people all over the world. This bridge has found its recognition and significance in several movies and photographs. This is a well known destination for the tourist to take a look at its historical carvings on support towers of this bridge. It is basically a suspension bridge that crosses the river of Thames near the Tower of London. The bridge is supported at the two ends by the towers and the design of this tower gives a vintage look to the Tower Bridge. One would see an exceptional scene when a ship passes by the river Thames. The bridge opens itself when a ship passes through the river Thames. The roads of the Tower Bridge are blocked and the bridge is opened from the middle to allow the ship pass to pass by. This gives a wonderful and a magnificent experience to all the tourists who visit this place at the time of spring.

Buckingham Palace

It is a heritage house located in London. It is an office house still today. There are 775 rooms in the palace and the building, built in 1837, is still in a condition that can challenge to the newly built houses of great attention. This is an administrative office still now and thus is one of the top places in London to be visited. You will not be able to visit all the rooms in the place, but you can easily manage the visit to top 450 rooms in the building and those 50 rooms are more than enough for the travelers. There are three important things in the palace. Many of the tour planners put this one out. Make sure that this is included in the spots as this is one of the top places to be visited in the city.

Palace of Westminster

It is the city house and is the parliament of the city too. The most important thing that you will get from the city house is the large interface of the place and the perfect design of it. This one of the oldest house of London and is the parliament of the place too. The best thing in the place is the view of that in the night sky. This is really a travel attraction, and especially from the banks of the Thames. This is the superb house that you will have to view and thus do not miss the place at any cost. Get the order from the court to visit the p-lace. If you are travelling with a trip planner, they will do the same for you.

Churchill War Rooms

Winston Churchill the then Prime Minister of The Great Britain, after declaring the war on Germany during Second World War moved into the bunkers which were called War Rooms. Presently these were converted into imperial war museums where one can find all the relics of World War – II. You can experience how Churchill faced the war through his documents and interviews. The cabinet room holds the Map Room and Telephonic Room which is Transatlantic. You can also watch a 15 min A/V on Churchill's life which contains some pictures and film clips of his political regime. It will be very interesting spot to hang on for the new visitors.

St. James Park

Being located at the heart of the city, St. James Park is surrounded by Buckingham Palace, The Mall, Horse Guards and Birdcage Walk one in each direction. It has got a lake and two islands one being the West Island and the other Duck Island. The Pelicans colony attracts everyone's attention. To have a perfect view of Buckingham Palace one needs to just stand on a blue colored bridge across the lake. With many buildings like the Horse Guards building, the Old War Office building, Whitehall Court, Foreign and Commonwealth Office and so on this park has attained its importance since times immemorial. This park gives the feeling of being in the homeland!

Royal Opera

Royal Opera meaning a theatre where various cultures of arts were performed is one of the major attractions in London. This huge building is otherwise called as 'Covent Garden' is the home for The Royal Opera, The Royal Ballet and the Orchestra. The House holds a capacity of 2,256 to its full strength comprising four tier boxes besides balconies and the amphitheatre gallery. This has become world's leading opera companies under the direction of Antonio Pappano. The great singers like the Anna Netrebko, Joyce DiDonato, Placido Domingo, Renee Fleming, Juan Diego Florez and many more had performed on this stage. To all those who got vexed up with sightseeing this gives a complete new energy!

Westminster Abbey

This is the most historical place one must visit which is situated close to the Houses of Parliament. Except Edward V and Edward VIII every Royal coronation took place in this Abbey. It had achieved the status of a Cathedral during the period of 1540 to 1556. Looking at the structure one can see the mightiness of this Abbey. As of now it is being used as a burial ground with as many as 3300 people being buried! One can find the cremations of great people like Sir Isaac Newton, Charles Darwin and so on. Due to the less space available we can find upright coffins here! An interesting fact is that a new museum and gallery is going to come up in this Abbey.

Hyde Park

The most visited parks of the London; Hyde Park is 350 acres in area comprising Princess of Wales Memorial Fountain, the Diana, Speakers' Corner and Serpentine Lake. If you are a family of five with naughty children then this place serves you better as it is stuffed with many recreational activities like the swimming, cycling, boating, tennis and even horse riding! In addition to these one can witness the fabulous 5k, 10k runs and the BBC's proms and live radio. Fact is that this park was built by Henry VIII for hunting it seems!

Chapter 4. Bars and Restaurants

London has now raised its level in the Gastro charts owing to its vast variety of food. This makes London a dream destination for those who live to eat! A big credit of the vibrant food culture goes to the fact that London has welcomed people around the world to be its citizens. These people have brought their own culture including cuisines to this lovely city they call "home".

There are few notable names of the restaurants that shine among the crowd and are a must go if you care to dig into some sumptuous delights.

JINJUU: Made from the kitchen of celebrity chef this notably serves the best Korean food ever – with Kimchin Fries and different pancakes.

Cereal Killer Café: The café offers 120 diverse cereals all around the earth all along with 30 dissimilar variety of milk, all adjacent to a milieu of 80s and 90s.

Spring : Amazing décor often attract foodies across the London area, kids, families and other people love to hang out from other areas due to its complete setup

Barrafina: Located on Soho's beside Firth Street just opened in the year 2007 and won 1st Michelin star just this last September month.

Bunga Bunga : Its wild karaoke nights is mostly appreciated from all around the world; a must-try experience

Chiltern Fire House: The Grade II gothic Victorian structure has been completely refurbished to include a high roof, huge mirrors and a completely open kitchen. This is the best time to book for the delicious lazy Monday lunch

Chicken Shop: - Free amazing and different variety of chicken dishes and recipes. It is a favorite haunt of the teens and you can find flocks of them hanging around here.

Hixter Bankside: This is undoubtedly an award winning space as termed – Marks bars and also a place for private party.

Gallery Mess: They boast of the various ranges of grilled dishes and amazing variety of seafood.

Top Dog: - the menu here is a hot favorite amongst kids; it delivers a wide variety of delicious hot dogs, different bread that are indeed special and amazing.

The Savoy hotel

The Savoy's American Bar was helpful in advancing the mixed drink – eternally famous beverages. Clients who usually visit would notice the group's dedicating for mixing drinks for its consumers.

Edition London: Punch Room

The name suggests that this bar's specialist packs a prolific punch and patrons definitely agree!

The Connaught hotel

For those who stay in London and love their drinks, they would surely know how lovely and grand the atmosphere of this awesome place is. The bar's menu includes number of multifarious and complex combinations that are unique to this place.

Claridge's Bar and the Fumoir;

The focus at the Claridge's Bar is its Vintage champagnes, rather than the cocktails. Designed by

David Collins, It serves a range of cocktails inspired specifically by 1930's era.

Dukes Hotel

Duke's purpose of qualification is its martinis. The bar's Italian supervisor Alessandro Palazzi is viewed as something of a martini maestro by the Martini enthusiasts. After a round or two of martinis, patrons are encouraged to rest in the lodging's patio nursery with a cognac and stogie.

Chapter 5. Night Life in London

London is amongst the cosmopolitan destinations of the world and therefore the nightlife and music scene here is quite impressive. There are numerous night clubs and that has made this place a perfect destination among the party revelers. There are some high end clubs and discotheques here where it is common to rub shoulders with some famous Hollywood celebrities. There are times when you would be lucky to find that the place is loaded with the star Rugby players of the state.

Make way to **Fabric** for this is one place that hosts its in-house talent and also brings in emerging musical talent from all around the world. The party here lasts all night and the focus is on good music. You want to indulge and splurge on your wild night out? Then **Notting Hill Arts Club** is for you. Known for being pricey and hosting young and vibrant crowd, this club is located in the suave West London. Housed in the old Camden Theatre, **KOKO** has made a big name for itself as a place that plays great music and gives platform to the best music talent around. There is a roof terrace, balconies and plush interiors that make KOKO, the place to be! **Mahiki** is one place which has had its fair share of hosting the younger generation of British Royal family! Amongst the patrons here are many A-listers who throng this place quite regularly. While there, do try their famous cocktails that they make like no one else does! An informal atmosphere with loads of music that goes from live gigs to Djs spinning some amazing sounds, **The Rhythm factory** is a great place to chill over drinks and dance like no one's watching! A brand of nightclubs that has made its mark throughout the world has one of its most happening clubs right here in the heart of London- **The Ministry of Sound.** It has music that makes the world sway and the talent that performs here has to be heard to be believed!

Chapter 6. Shopping in The City of London

Shopping in London can be an amazing experience for you, on your trip to this place. There are too many options available for you and the interesting point about shopping in London is there are a few places which have a unique specialty or theme. The best option you have when you are on a trip to London is looking for the city center shopping malls. They are preferred more by everyone because you will be able to shop everything under one roof. You don't have to look for a different shopping something else. You also have facilities like lunch, coffee, dinner at these shopping malls and hence you can spend as much time as you want in the shopping. A few shopping malls offer you entertainment facilities like cinemas, children's facilities, etc. Here are a few shopping malls for you to shop when you are in London. Westfield London shopping mall, The Mall Wood Green, Box Park Shoredicth, Stratford center, Whiteleys, Ealing Broadway shopping mall, Victoria Palace, The Plaza, Angel Central, Lewisham Shopping center, Kings Mall Shopping center, One New Change and many more. You have unlimited options to shop in London.

Chapter 7. Hotels in London

London hosts the most important conventions since it is the financial district of Europe. Not to forget its preferred destination tag by tourists, there is always a steady stream of visitors to this city all-round the year. Whatever be the purpose, a business summit or knowing the city better, London provides a wide range of accommodation options to those who choose to visit this alluring city.

There are many budget hotels and they are perfect for low budget traveler, backpackers and big families. Amongst the star properties, the Dorchester and the Savoy are well-known names. There are hundreds of hotels and out of them there are more than 20 that are five star graded and over a 100 that are best for the budget boarders. Most of the hotels provide the support of online booking. Thus get to the websites and book the hotel rooms, before you visit the place. This will make it easier for you to plan your travel.

Final Words

This city is such a mix of colors and cultures that even a tourist feels home while exploring this magnificent city. Every turn here holds a surprise and every time you look up, there stands an architectural marvel in front of you. So plan your trip today to the city where visual marvels never cease and night never ends.

Thank You Page

I want to personally thank you for reading my book. I hope you found information in this book useful and I would be very grateful if you could leave your honest review about this book. I certainly want to thank you in advance for doing this.

If you have the time, you can check my other books too.

www.ingramcontent.com/pod-product-compliance
Lightning Source LLC
LaVergne TN
LVHW021745060526
838200LV00052B/3484